GET CODING
WITH
REPEATING

What are loops and why do coders need them? Find out with fun puzzles and games!

Kevin Wood

WINDMILL BOOKS ™

New York

Published in 2018 by **Windmill Books**, An Imprint of Rosen Publishing
29 East 21st Street, New York, NY 10010

Produced for Windmill Books by Alix Wood Books
Designed by Alix Wood
Editor: Eloise Macgregor
Editor for Windmill Books: Kerri O'Donnell

Photo credits: Cover background © Shutterstock; All robot artwork © Adobe Stock Images and Alix Wood;
all other art © Alix Wood

CATALOGING-IN-PUBLICATION DATA

Names: Wood, Kevin.
Title: Get coding with repeating / Kevin Wood.
Description: New York : Windmill Books, 2018. | Series: Computer-free coding | Includes index.
Identifiers: ISBN 9781499482591 (pbk.) | ISBN 9781499482553 (library bound) | ISBN 9781499482485 (6 pack)
Subjects: LCSH: Computer programming--Juvenile literature. | Programming languages (Electronic computers)--
    Juvenile literature.
Classification: LCC QA76.6 W66 2018 | DDC 005.1--dc23

Printed in the United States of America

CPSIA compliance information: Batch # BS17WM: For further information contact Gareth Stevens, New York, New York at 1-800-542-2595.

Contents

Code and Loops

We tell computers what to do by writing them instructions known as code. Computers will do exactly what you tell them to do. Even though they can seem really smart, they are actually just following orders. It is the coders who are smart! Sometimes the instructions can get pretty long and repetitive. That's why loops are useful.

WHAT IS A LOOP?

Loops help you write code that tells a computer to do the same thing several times. Why is that useful? Say we wanted to get the yellow robot, Sleebot, to blink his eyes ten times. We would need to tell him to open his eyes and shut his eyes ten times. Look at the code on the right. It's pretty long and hard to read. The loop below is much simpler.

```
OpenEyes
ShutEyes    x 10
```

OpenEyes
ShutEyes
OpenEyes
ShutEyes
OpenEyes
ShutEyes
OpenEyes
ShutEyes
OpenEyes
ShutEyes
OpenEyes
ShutEyes
OpenEyes
ShutEyes
OpenEyes
ShutEyes
OpenEyes
ShutEyes
OpenEyes
ShutEyes

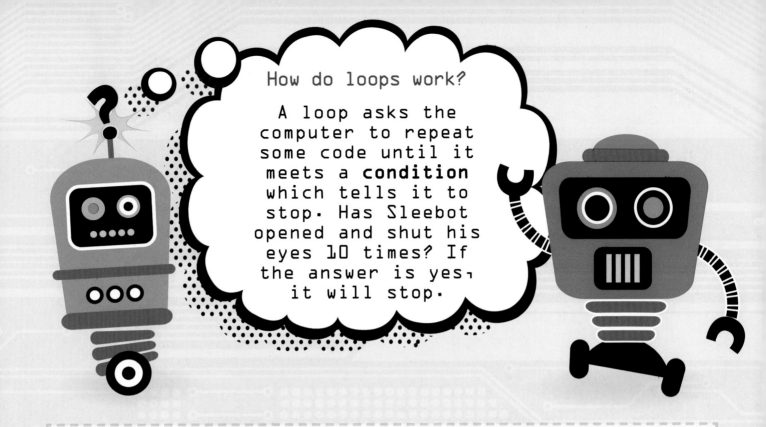

How do loops work?

A loop asks the computer to repeat some code until it meets a **condition** which tells it to stop. Has Sleebot opened and shut his eyes 10 times? If the answer is yes, it will stop.

GET Programming

This code programs a robot to walk around in a square. Which part of this code would be better if we used a loop?

WalkTenPaces_Turn90**Degrees**

WalkTenPaces_Turn90Degrees

WalkTenPaces_Turn90Degrees

WalkTenPaces_Stop

Which of the loops below could we use in our program?

a) WalkTenPaces Turn90Degrees × 4

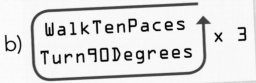

b) WalkTenPaces Turn90Degrees × 3

Answers are on page 32

Types of Loop

There are several different types of loop. They all work in slightly different ways. The main difference between types of loop is when they stop looping.

A loop stops when it reaches its **terminating condition**. Terminating just means stopping. When Sleebot the robot was programmed to open and shut his eyes on page 4, the terminating condition the code had to meet was "x 10." Once the loop had happened ten times, the loop stopped. This kind of loop is called a "For Loop," because it happens for a certain number of times.

What exactly is a condition?

A condition is something agreed on or necessary before some other thing can happen. It's like your mom saying, "You can go play on one condition: you've done your homework."

What if you wanted your loop to happen just while something else was happening, and then stop when that event stopped? This kind of loop is known as a "While Loop." Perhaps you wanted to program a bird to fly around just while you were clapping your hands:

```
WhileIAmClapping
FlyAroundTheRoom
```

When you stop clapping your hands, the code then reaches its terminating condition. The bird will stop flying.

ENDLESS LOOPS

Another kind of loop is known as an "Endless Loop" or "Forever Loop." As you can guess from the names, these loops never stop looping. This is either because they do not have a terminating condition, or the condition can never be met, or the condition tells the loops to repeat.

Which of the conditions below would cause an endless loop? Why?

a) Set Value to 3.
End Loop if Value Is Less Than 4.

b) Set Value to 5.
End Loop if Value Is Less Than 4.

Even endless loops aren't forever. They end when the program shuts down or you turn the computer off.

Answers are on page 32

All About While Loops

In computing we often use the words "if" and "then" together. For example, if I clap my hands, then fly. This if/then code would mean that the bird stops flying between each clap. The bird would be up and down like a yo- yo! That was probably not what you wanted your code to do.

WHILE LOOPS

A While Loop would help! While Loops tell the computer to keep doing something based on a condition. In this case, the condition is clapping. Here is a **flowchart** of what a While Loop looks like:

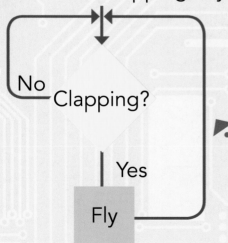

While I am Clapping, Fly

No — Clapping?

Yes

Fly

CODING TIPS

While Loops must keep asking if their condition has been met.

Are you still clapping? Yes or no? If yes, fly. If no, don't fly.

Each cycle around the question is known as an **iteration**. The result of one iteration (yes or no) is then used as the starting point for the next iteration.

One journey around this loop is known as an iteration.

GET Programming

Could you create your own While Loop? Think of an everyday task that you do where you look for a condition to tell you that you should stop. How about walking up the stairs? While you are on the stairs, you keep climbing. If you reach the top and there are no more stairs, you stop climbing. Otherwise, you'd look silly! Draw your own loop, like this one.

While Stair Is In Front Of Me, Climb

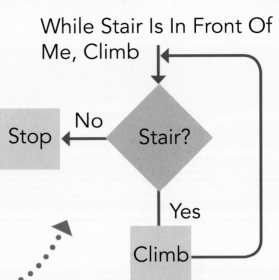

There is another loop that works in a similar way to a While Loop, known as an Until Loop. A While Loop asks the question at the start of the code, and an Until Loop asks the question at the end.

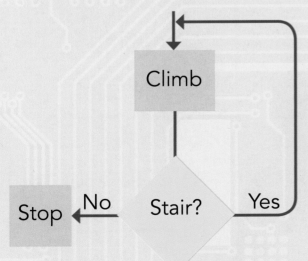

Can you see the difference between While Loops and Until Loops?

Look at the diagram. Using an Until Loop, you would do one last climb before you asked if there was a stair. That would look silly!

9

What Do For Loops Do?

For Loops are one of the most common types of loops used in code. The For Loop is useful because it can count! You can tell a For Loop to do something a certain number of times. If you were writing code for a robot to walk up stairs, and you knew the number of stairs, your code could use a For Loop. You would tell the robot to "ClimbStair" for that number of times. The value (the number of stairs) is known as a **variable**.

ClimbStair
x 2

What exactly is
a variable?

Data that may
change is known
as a variable.
Variables can be
numbers or words.

VARIABLE?

Which of these is
the variable?

a)   Climb

b)   Stair

c)   2

Answers are on page 32

CODE THAT COUNTS

For Loops allow the computer to keep a count of how many times it has done something. It does this by adding 1 to the value each time it goes around the loop. To write code to make a robot climb 5 steps, the code would need to keep count. The loop adds 1 to the previous count, so your code keeps track of what number it has gotten to.

```
ClimbSteps
Count is 1
Add 1
Count is 2
Add 1
Count is 3
Add 1
Count is 4
Add 1
Count is 5
End
```

GET Programming

Try this looping game. Gather some friends. Someone stands up and shouts "1." Then they point to the next person who must add one to the variable and shout out that number. That person stands and shouts out "2." Keep playing until you get to 10. Mix it up by doing a dance move or jumping jack instead of just standing.

In code terms, our loop has declared a variable and set it to 1. The code then commands the person to stand (or dance or do a jumping jack) and say the variable value for each time around the loop. They add one to the variable each time and stop when it is at 10.

The code might look something like this. This is **pseudocode**. "Pseudo" means "pretend." All coding languages look a little different. You'll learn different ways to write a loop depending which language you are using.

```
StandAndShoutNumbers
StartValue = 1
StopValue = 10

StandAndShoutValue
Add 1
```

More For Loops

Sometimes, you don't want your loop to go up in ones. With For Loops you can start when you want, end when you want, and increase by whatever number you want. Try playing the "For Loop Hopscotch" game below.

GET Programming

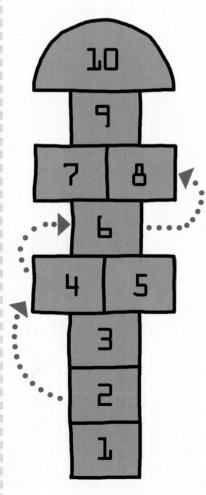

Draw a hopscotch grid, like the one pictured on the left, with chalk on the sidewalk. Ask a friend to choose a start square, a stop square, and how many squares at a time you have to jump. Here's an example:

Start at 2
Stop at 9
Jump 2 squares

Stand on the "Start" number square. Add 2 to the number of the square you are on. Hop to that square. Keep going until you reach or would go beyond your "Stop" square.

Did you get to square 9 or did you have to stop before you got there? How many times did you hop? Try it with some new numbers.

Answers are on page 32

LOOPY DANCING

There are a lot of things that we do in everyday life that could be written as a For Loop. Think about dancing. We often repeat the same moves in a loop when we dance. Try this loopy hand jive routine!

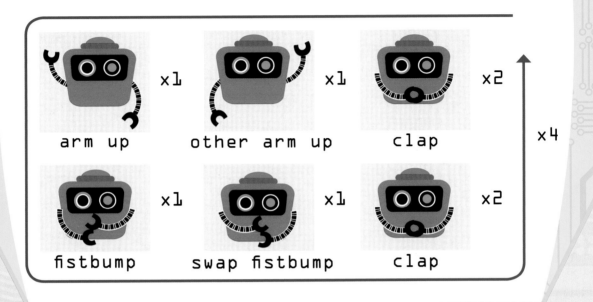

Variables can be counters, like in the code above. They can also be **accumulators**. Accumulators are variables that the code uses to make calculations. They work just like when you add a few numbers together in your head. Say you had to add 4+2+1. You would add 4+2 first, which is 6. Six would be the accumulator variable. You would hold that number in your head to do the next part of the problem, 6 + 1.

CODING TIPS

One easy way to understand the difference between a counter and an accumulator is to think of the variables like a bunch of coins. If you were asked to count the coins below, you would count the number of coins you had (3). If you were asked for the accumulated value of the coins, you would add their values together (5+5+1 = 11).

Endless Loops just keep looping. They are not often used on purpose in coding. Usually they occur when the code has a mistake. You may have a **bug** in your code! A bug is what coders call a mistake in a program. It is easy to make mistakes when you write code. Everyone does!

GETTING RID OF BUGS

When coders search through and find any problems in their code, it is called **debugging**. When they find the mistake, they change that part of code and then run it to test that it now works how they expected it to. If it still doesn't, they need to look again.

What do bugs look like?

Bugs can be simple typing mistakes or errors in the order the code is written. Sometimes a bug happens because the coder's thinking is a little off.

ENDLESS BUGS

An Endless Loop may happen when a loop's terminating condition is never met, so the loop can never stop. A coder may have accidentally typed in a wrong number. Or they may not have thought through what the code should be looking for. This means that the computer could be constantly looking for something that it will never find.

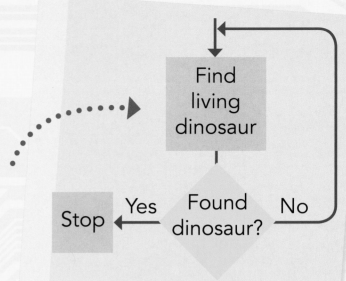

GET Programming

Can you see why the following two pieces of code would become Endless Loops?

1.
```
Look For the
Letter "A" in
the word "Code"
```

2.
```
Add 0 to 0.
If total greater
than 1, end loop
```

Which of the changes below would fix these two bugs?

3. a) change the letter "A" to one of the letters in the word code.

   b) change the word "Code" to "Cone."

4. c) change the problem to Add 0 to 1.

   d) change the problem to Add 1 to 1.

Answers are on page 32

Breaking a Loop

Sometimes you might want to break out of a loop before it is complete. This is usually because a certain condition is met.

Say you want to keep riding your bike around the block until sunset, but then break the loop if the ice cream truck arrives.

You need to add two conditions to your loop. You need to ask "Sun Up?" If the answer is "yes," you continue on your loop. You also need to ask the question "Ice Cream Truck?" If the answer is "yes," you can break out of the loop.

BikeAroundTheBlock

No

Sun Up?

Break

Yes

Yes

Ice Cream Truck?

No

Bike

SNAKE EYES

Try this game. You will need two dice. Each player throws the two dice and adds their score together, 10 times. This is your loop. This is what your loop might look like written in code.

The person with the highest score at the end wins.

If anyone throws two 1s (snake eyes), the game is over for that player. This is your break. This is what your break might look like written inside the loop.

```
Set your score to 0
Do 10 times {
    Throw the dice
    Add the sum of the
    dice to your score
}
What is your score?
```

Here, these curly brackets mark the beginning and end of a loop.

```
Do 10 times {
    Throw the dice
    If the dice show two 1s
- STOP, GAME OVER
    Add the sum of the
    dice to your score
}
What is your score?
```

How many different conditions can you have in a loop?

As many as you like!

17

Shortening Your Code

One of the best things about loops is they make your code shorter and easier to read. They also save time when you write out your code. A loop can change a long list of commands into a much shorter single command.

MAKE IT SHORTER

The instructions on the right side of this page tell the robot to walk around the pond. How could you make the code shorter and simpler?

```
WalkNorthOneStep
WalkNorthOneStep
WalkNorthOneStep
WalkEastOneStep
WalkEastOneStep
WalkEastOneStep
WalkNorthOneStep
WalkNorthOneStep
WalkNorthOneStep
WalkNorthOneStep
WalkNorthOneStep
JumpOverStream
WalkWestOneStep
WalkWestOneStep
WalkWestOneStep
SitOnBench
```

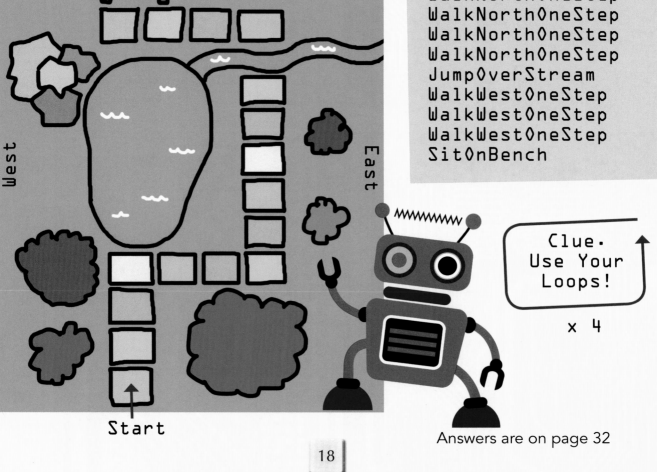

North

West

East

Start

Clue.
Use Your
Loops!

x 4

Answers are on page 32

GET Programming

You can write loop code for patterns. Can you spot a pattern in this row of cupcakes? Which of the loops below would show a friend how to put the cupcakes in the same order, a, b, or c?

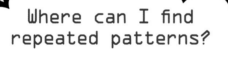

a)   x3

b)   x3

c)   x4

Answer is on page 32

Where can I find repeated patterns?

Wallpaper and curtain designs often have a repeat pattern. See if you can find one.

CODING TIPS

Mistakes are less likely when you use loops because the code is shorter. Bugs are easier to fix, too, because you would only have to change an error once inside the loop.

If you had written all the commands over and over, you would have to fix the error everywhere it was typed. That would take a lot longer and you'd be more likely to make a mistake.

Subroutines

Sometimes you may want to repeat chunks of code but don't need them to loop. Perhaps you have written some code telling your robot how to pick apples from a tree. Every time the robot sees an apple, you want to run that bit of code, but you don't want to have to type it out every time. You can make a **subroutine**, and call it PickApple.

To write a subroutine you need to give it a name, so you can call for it when you want to run it. We'll call ours PickApple.

```
PickApple
    LiftArm
    GrabApple
    Pull
    PutAppleInBasket
    This is a subroutine ◀····
```

We need to tell the computer that our code is a subroutine. Then we can call for it by name. Different computer languages have different ways to call for a subroutine. You might type "GOSUB PickApple" or something similar.

CODING TIPS

If you keep your subroutines simple and general, sometimes you can use the same subroutine for different programs. Perhaps you want to display a user's name on screen. You could write a subroutine and use the same one in several programs.

"Hello Jim"

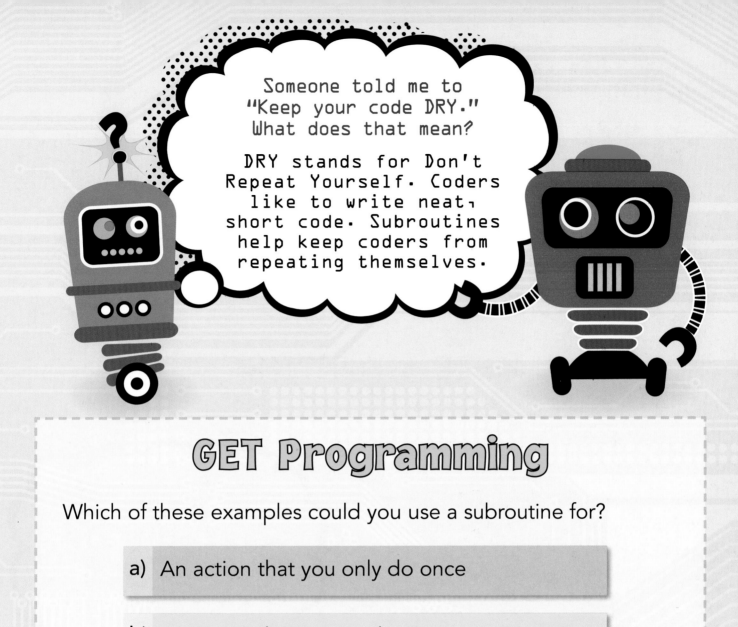

Someone told me to "Keep your code DRY." What does that mean?

DRY stands for Don't Repeat Yourself. Coders like to write neat, short code. Subroutines help keep coders from repeating themselves.

GET Programming

Which of these examples could you use a subroutine for?

a) An action that you only do once

b) An action that you might want to repeat

c) An action that you might do in a loop

Answers are on page 32

You can run the same subroutine as many times as you like. You just call for it by name in your code.

Using Functions

Another way to repeat code is by using **functions**. Functions and subroutines are similar. The main difference is a function will give you a result. For example, you might write a function that multiplies anything given to it by 2. It would figure out the answer and give you the result.

HOW DO YOU WRITE A FUNCTION?

Just as with subroutines, you must first name your function. You can then call it by name when you want to use it. We could call our function "MultiplyBy2." Then we must follow the name with a set of parentheses ( ) where we put the **parameter**, or the number we want to multiply by 2.

a = MultiplyBy2(3)
a = 6

Do functions only do math?

No, a function might ask for some words to be typed in. It would give you those words as the result.

CODING TIPS

Computer programs have lots of functions that are already written for you. You may not have to write your own unless you want something really particular to your program.

If you just want to use a ready-made function in a program, you don't have to know how it works. It's sort of like when you watch TV—you don't have to know how the TV works to be able to use it.

The only time you need to know how a function works is if you need to write the function yourself or change how it works. Just like with the TV, you would only have to know how it worked if you had to build one or fix one.

GET Programming

Try playing this game with a friend. You will need a book. The purpose of your function is to get a result from a given page number, line number, and word number. We'll call the function FindWord. Say you want your friend to go to page 5, line 6, word 4. You would write:

a = FindWord(5,6,4)
a = (write the word you found here)

Take turns to find the words. When you have found six words, see if you can make a sentence out of them. It's not always possible! Can you make a sentence out of these words?

In   Repeat   Don't   Yourself   Code

Answers are on page 32

Event Loops

An Event Loop is a loop that waits for something to happen and then reacts to it. Event Loops are constantly testing to see whether the event they are waiting for has happened.

DIRECTING TRAFFIC

Event Loops catch events as they happen and then give them to a **handler**. The handler will then perform whatever function we have programmed.

What kind of event is an Event Loop looking for?

An event could be a user typing a key, clicking a mouse, or swiping on a touchscreen.

CODING TIPS

Event Loops don't just look for mouse clicks or touchscreen swipes. They may also look for signals from sensors in the computer. For example, sensors checking the battery level of a laptop may trigger an event when the battery gets low. Perhaps it will send the user a message letting them know.

low battery

GET Programming

Imagine the human body is like a big computer. It is running all the time, breathing in and breathing out. It is also looking out for events it should react to. Look at the flowchart below:

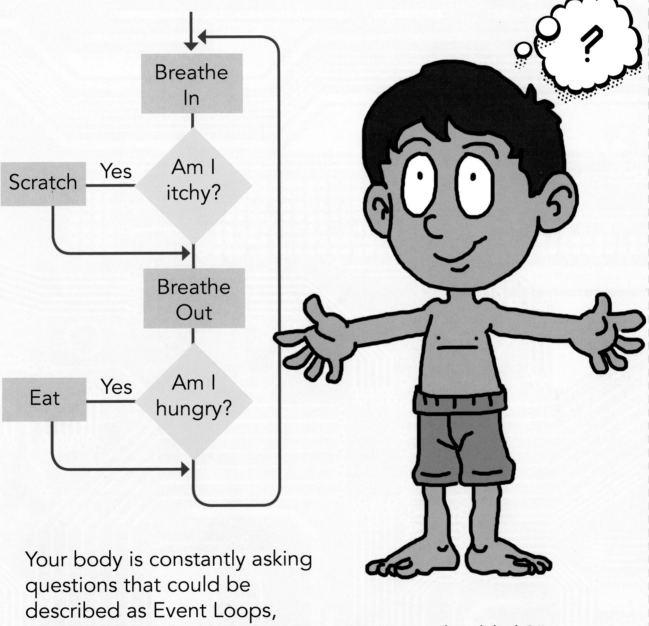

Your body is constantly asking questions that could be described as Event Loops, such as "Can I feel any pain?" or "Do I need to blink?" It tells the right part of the body to react to the situations. Can you think of any more? Draw yourself a flowchart!

Nested Loops

There can even be a loop inside another loop! The inside loop is known as a Nested Loop. You would use a Nested Loop if you wanted something to repeat itself inside an action that also repeats itself.

L ◊LOOP◊ P

Imagine you had a cleaning robot. You might want your robot to push the vacuum across your bedroom four times. Each time he crosses the room, you might also want him to stop and wave his arms three times, to get rid of cobwebs. The arm-waving would be a Nested Loop.

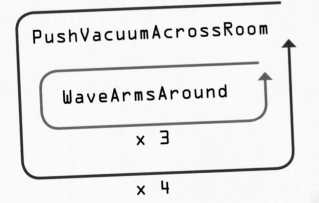

```
PushVacuumAcrossRoom

  WaveArmsAround

      x 3

                x 4
```

HOW DO NESTED LOOPS WORK?

With Nested Loops, the inner loop has to complete its task before the outer loop can start its loop again. Nested Loops work a little like a clock. A clock has three loops. The inner loop is the second hand. It is surrounded by the minute hand. The hour hand is the outer loop.

Only after the second hand completes its iteration (gone once around the clockface) can the minute hand start its iteration and move to the next minute. The hour hand must wait for the minute hand to complete its loop around the clockface before it can move to the next hour.

LOOP OR NOT?

Which of these examples might use a Nested Loop?

a) Walk back and forth across a bridge three times. Stop halfway and catch two fish.

b) Keep juggling three balls until you drop one.

Answers are on page 32

Can You Pass the Test?

1. What is a terminating condition?
   a) not feeling very well
   b) a condition that stops a loop
   c) a condition that says you'll be back

2. If you wanted a loop to do something a certain number of times, which loop would you use?
   a) a For Loop b) a While Loop c) a Forever Loop

3. What is an iteration?
   a) one journey around a loop
   b) an error in the coding of a loop

4. Which of these describes a variable?
   a) data that may change
   b) a robot
   c) a computer language

5. What is debugging?
   a) checking your machine for insects
   b) removing old files from your computer
   c) finding problems in your code and fixing them

6. Which of these things do loops do to your code?
   a) make it longer
   b) make it shorter

I think I got
some right!
Did you?

7. What does DRY stand for?
   a) Don't Repeat Yourself
   b) Didn't Run Yet

8. Which of these are parentheses?
   a) < >   b) ( )   c) { }

9. Which of these might trigger
   an event loop?
   a) pressing a key on the keyboard
   b) a mouse click
   c) a timer
   d) all of the above

10. What is a nested loop?
    a) a loop inside another loop
    b) a loop that has been completed

Turn this page upside down to see the answers.

Quiz Answers

1. b) a condition that stops a loop; 2. a) a For Loop; 3. a) one journey around a loop; 4. a) data that may change; 5. c) finding problems in your code and fixing them; 6. b) make it shorter; 7. a) Don't Repeat Yourself; 8. b) ( ); 9. d) all of the above; 10. a) a loop inside another loop

Glossary

accumulators Variables that the code uses to make calculations.

bug An unexpected mistake or imperfection in computer code.

condition Something essential to the occurrence of something else.

debugging Finding and removing mistakes in a computer program.

degrees A unit of measure for angles that is equal to an angle with its vertex at the center of a circle and its sides cutting off 1/360 of the circumference.

flowchart A graphic representation of a logic sequence

functions Procedures or routines done on a computer that produce a result.

handler A software routine that performs a particular task.

iteration A computational process in which a series of operations is repeated a number of times.

parameter A special kind of variable, used in a subroutine to refer to one of the pieces of data.

pseudocode A notation used in program design resembling a simplified programming language.

subroutine A set of instructions designed to perform a frequently used operation within a program.

terminating condition A condition that causes a process to stop.

variable Data that can change and may take on any one of a set of values.

BOOKS

Hubbard, Ben. *How Coding Works*. Chicago, IL: Heinemann-Raintree, 2017.

Saujani, Reshma. *Girls Who Code: Learn to Code and Change the World*. New York, NY: Viking Books, 2017.

For web resources related to the subject of this book, go to:
www.windmillbooks.com/ weblinks
and select this book's title.

Index

Answers

page 5: b

page 7: b; the condition can never be met.

page 10: c

page 12: You should have ended up on square 8, stopping before you got to square 9. You should have hopped 3 times.

page 15: 1. There is no letter "A" in "Code"; 2. The total of 0 and 0 can never be greater than 1; 3. a; 4. d

page 18: WalkNorthOneStep x 3
WalkEastOneStep x 3
WalkNorthOneStep x 5
JumpOverStream
WalkWestOneStep x 3
SitOnBench

page 19: b

page 21: b

page 23: Don't Repeat Yourself In Code, or In Code Don't Repeat Yourself

page 27: a